Never Chosen

a journey of love without love

by kerline dieudonne

sketches by chris harris
"wake up" by ralph ingrassia

Published by
Mind State
Covington, GA 30016

All rights reserved. No part of this book may be reproduced, scanned, or distributed in any print or electronic form without permission from the publisher, except where permitted by law. Piracy of copyrighted materials is a violation of the author's rights

Published by Mind State
ISBN: 978-0-6151-7743-4
Copyright © 2007

All rights reserved.

For the times I wasn't the one and for the times I could have been, but I was never chosen. I thank my lucky stars that I was chosen for that. Love is a complicated animal that you can only attempt to tame, do it wisely.

May love fall upon you and you are chosen

≈

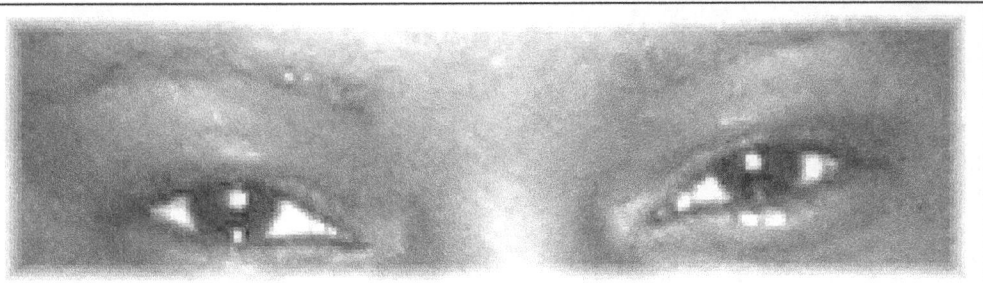

the introduction

my name is kerline they use to call me goldy because my heart was made of pure gold but someone stole it.

i found it and took it back

scared to lose it again i wrapped the gold around each lock of hair on my head

but you don't know me though, because i haven't written those lines
those sade isn't it a crime lines,

i'm not a native son like richard wright
maya angelou knows why the caged bird sings,

i on the other hand like achebe knows that things fall apart
so like alicia keys, you don't know my name...but you will!

de l'amour

7

it ain't real

he tells me he loves me
but it ain't real

i feel him beside me
yet i can not feel

when night has escaped me,
the tears i cannot conceal
he tells me he loves me
and inside me he wants to feel

lost by his words
broken by his touch
i am there only to satisfy his lust

a tear finds its way and it breaks free
and in his twisted mind, he's satisfied me
he kisses my forehead,
no more is said

he tells me he loves me and i go to bed

in his hands

i think of him, not just him but also his hands

thank God for those hands

but his hands would be nothing without those arms, strong and steady
which are carried by beautiful broad shoulders

just the thought of his lips drive me insane, the way they gently caress my skin
never leaving one breast more envious than the other, or the way they are eager to please me

not just his lips but also his chest
so strong and tempting, my hands can't keep away

my lips want to taste and my body wants to be close

there is one part of him that i always think of the most but i won't say

but if you think about the sweetest thing you could ever taste,
the warmest, yet most comfortable day that God has ever made
a meal that has satisfied you
the quenching of your thirst
a slow release of air before your lungs burst

you still wouldn't come close to understanding what i feel when i think of him

the feel of him inside me, just the thought makes me sweat
when he moves in deeper and i start to get really wet he moans so soft
like a small breath of air telling me he's not finished yet

he moves me where he wants me
bends me until i am pleased
twist me how he feels
carefully, with the utmost ease taking heed of my needs

i think of him in the morning
before the wake of the sun
even in the evening
when the work of the sun is done
in the mid evening night and in the dusk of dawn
i'll think of him always
not just his chest, lips, arms, or shoulder

but what he makes me feel like when i'm in his hands

the last

i am the last of a dying breed
an infectious collection of soil and seed
roots that twine, wine and bind with the
knowledge that the warmth of the day and
sunlight will bare fruits of wisdom

with folds of lavender, that are soft
lips of honey, that are sweet
a touch of power, that is strong
a breed that birds sing in song

yes i am the last of a dying breed

sand with grains hard to the touch
small to the human eye
with straw, long and firm
brittle but subtle

i am clay

molded to perfection,
not limited to style or selection
crafted with ease
craved with skill
the last with this courage for will

thorn with hurt
filled with the blood of pain
personified by love
fear coursing through veins

i am conscious

subtle desires of passion
pleasure gone pain
the gentle cry of my name
brushes against my lips

16

hands embrace hips
deep pushes and moist breathes
moving in shifts

i am excitement

a forgotten moment,
being forgotten,
fruit grown half eaten,
half rotten

last of a breed

i am human

i never said it

i never said it but i felt it

it was an emotion flowing
through my body
that almost ate my soul

i still feel your hands warm on my skin
i still have your sweat on my pillow
from when we last made love

i haven't taken your clothes
out of my closet
and your pictures still adorn my wall

at night when i dream
i taste the salt of your tears
i hear the bellow of your cries
and i still feel your heart beating inside me
long after i'm awake

it has been two years now
i have watched the flowers grow
seen the fall of the snow
and all without you

two long years and i have never told you
but with all my heart i've felt it

i think it started the moment i met you
it must have been the way you looked at me
no!
perhaps your caress or hold on me
the touch of your lips so hard
and deep, you fell inside of me

your eyes
your nose
your mouth
your hair
your clothes
your stare

i wish these moments, recollections of you
would dissipate
become air then carried with the wind

i wish the night would cease bringing you
your memory
to my mind
my heart and my bed

it has been in my heart
lingering
like the sweetest tree
with roots that dig deep into the earth

it has always been there growing inside me
beating like a pulse
maybe i wasn't strong enough
proud enough
scared enough
loud enough
maybe i talked too much
cared too much
hurt too much or died just a touch

it's not important any more i know
but the days are long and nights even longer
life is too sweet and the hurt even stronger

my regrets are countless
and my hopes in number even larger
i gave without thinking
took without blinking
before i knew it i was thirsty and carried on without drinking

now i'm stronger
prouder
louder

no longer standing in the shadow of emotions
but still the taste of what was on my lips lingers
i never said it but you felt it

i never loved you

ananda's sixteen today

> her mother didn't notice the pain
> she was in
> when ananda sat down before a
> steaming plate
> of cod fish and plantain

she patted ananda's head and
persuaded her "eat, eat you need
your strength"
for her mother if she did not see it,
it was not there
perhaps it wasn't

> her mother thought of her own
> days of youth
> the life she once had
> of maids and private schools
> but most of all she pitied the life
> she now lived
> of corn meal and dry fish
> the man she loved with no love in
> return

she thought of everything except the
pain ananda
was going through, which was her own

> ananda's brother came home and
> mumbled
> "whats up?"
> no one replied, they simply
> nodded their heads
> i'm sure he saw the rain in her
> eyes
> but he was tired as well as broke
> all he thought of was the dime bag
> that he longed to smoke

he works hard for his
he don't ask for much
so why would he think of her eyes
when he can fill his with smoke

                    so ananda sat and ate her fish and
                    thought of God and this being her
                    final dish

i don't know why she hurt
was it the heart she could not mend?
the friends she could not confide in?
the dreams she did not have or the ones that were lost?
maybe inside she merely died

                    i don't know what hurt her so
                    but when she finished her last dish
                    she went upstairs, she said goodbye to her teddy bears
                    and she combed her pretty dark wooly hair

she took out the blade
she hid so well behind her eyes
ananda held her lips together tight
determine to release no air
or tears from her eyes

                    she tried to think of all the good nights she once had, but thought of the nights that
                    took her deep into the morning and woke her feeling bad

so that blade split her soft skin and
pierced her vein
through brown and red she kept digging
and digging
trying to rid herself of the pain

        ananda's sixteen today
        she sleeps in a meadow, a field of dreams
        along with her shame
        where her brother weeps with open eyes
        and her mother just a little bit
        every day learns to cry

call waiting

so you're telling me that my man doesn't
want me?

now he's yours
you're saying that he has plans for you
and him
marriage, and 4 children
that the darker the berry doesn't
sweeten the juice
that only a sister like you can make a
man bust his pockets loose

so you want me to know how well he's
feeling your flow?
what, did he smell your pussy?
get you wet?
stroke you hard?
ate you out?
you made him cum?

you're telling me that he never knew
beauty
until he knew your name
that loving me was a foreign object and
he was a brother you had to tame?

yeah!
your body is right, legs, chest, ass, you're
tight
yeah!

ok, ok
so what i'm kind of small... but hold on i have another call

ok what did you say?
yeah i am few shades from midnight
and straying too far from day...right?
oh yeah ok you got that, some ass i could use

but i don't have to make him choose and i don't have to claim him
but i do have to go, because the man that you said is no longer mine, is on the other line

all in one breath

like a body of water you surround me
an ocean of air, you move through me
the smell of you
feel of you
taste of you

like the dark holds mysteries you hold me
a symphony in the key of c
the piano you play is me

i reach for you, to touch you
in places you long to be touched
you move towards me, in me
between my thighs you take refuge

your lips taste me
 your hands know me
i feel you
and as if a dam has been broken
you plunge inside me
the moisture of my body on yours
pellets of sweat become an ocean
and you swim in me

thick as honey
dark as chocolate
sweeter than life its self
inside me

like the dark holds mysteries
you hold me
a symphony in the key of c
you play me
and i feel you all in one breath

this poem is not about love

i will not speak of love
i will not personify your hands that
stroke my form
there's no way i'll give light to the
gentle way you make me sway
the taste of you, drunk with love
corrupted my mind;
 i'd rather not speak of your kind

this poem is not about love!

hilltops covered with trees,
burgundy tinted skies with orange
that cry
i was green with envy to know that
she would be in your arms

scattered with one breath from God
some leaves blew and some fell
i guess i was the one to fall
you with the wind or perhaps God
went on
but i will not speak of love

cold nights you bury your head in her
breast
between her thighs and in passion
look deeply in her eyes
warm days strip naked and lay with
her heart in your arms
beating on your chest
do you thank God or me for leaving
you

i didn't know the cost of loving you
now that it's over, it's quite obvious that i do
thirsty for blood you struck my vein
and the taste of you drove me insane
i needed to feel complete and intact
to my dismay went back over and over again
you weren't only my lover but my beloved friend

i'd rather speak of the pounding of my heart
breathlessness of my soul
and the quiet soft cries in my mind
for love has never to me been kind
nor sweet like a summer filled with laughter birthing sunshine giving light to an old day turned new
it was you

you who whispered lies and added the sparkle in my eye
and in a glimpse like the move of the tide and as if you had the world to hide, were gone

so, no i won't speak of love

i'd rather speak of the hole that sits in my chest, the very place where love use to rest
the burnt flesh that i myself had to dress,
i want to talk about the baggage and the stress

not love
not the feeling of passion at its best
or the tender way we caress
that's not the issue i feel i need to address

i just want to know, why?

is it her laugh or her smile
that hurdled you into denial
the shape of her breast
or the touch of her that turned you into a child
what did she have that i could not give
and as if the world collided with the sun
a battle between good and evil she had won
and you were in her arms

no i will not speak of love

nor the pain that dwells inside
for if you were thinking of love,
love would have brought you home begging like a child
but i think of my pride so deep and so vile
no woman would cast a stone or scream in denial
a cry of ignorance and love hums quietly on the inside

i guess this poem is about me and what i expected love to be

can you hear them?

today bells rang
white and pink lace adorned little girls, even the smallest ones pranced tall as they paraded in the hall

this day was filled with sugar and cake
almonds covered with white powder
and coconut flakes a top of layers
and layers of cream filled yellow cake

this day marked a new, where day and night was settled by afternoon
where better or worse found common ground and all watched in a soft quite hush waiting to see if the foundation was sound

the bells rang out loud and strong
who would judge that this day was wrong, who would have known that the bells needed this, a confirmation of one single kiss
that the sun would dance when they have rung or that rivers of salt would flow when they are done

he seemed to love her when he did not know her with one stroke of his hand on her cheek he told her, he adored her a glance that only pure love can speak, with the words that old lovers teach

and the bells rang out

for better or for worse would she have to keep?
and he tried to love her but the bells have already rung, the pastor has given his blessing and the choir has sung
did you hear them?

now months have passed she was no longer
the one he remembered it was now april and
they only married in september
it seemed like the passion had gone and all
the things he loved about her was wrong

can you hear them?
the bells have rung the cake has
been cut and her hand has been won and he
tried to love her but the bells have already
rung, the pastor has given his blessing and
the choir has sung
did you hear them?

even though the sun danced when they rung,
rivers of salt flowed when they were done
and his love for her was confirmed with a
single kiss,   maybe this was not God's wish?
maybe it was in the kiss?

shhh...

to realize that he encompassed
my mind would have taken some
thought
if i could have noticed the fall
i was about to take,
he would have been caught
but i didn't
so he touched me

had things been different i would have
never let myself go
first by keeping my rules of saying no
but it was so good when it was good
and so he touched me

now i sit and i try to separate the
passion,
but the feeling is lasting
if i realized
noticed
caught him
oh! if things had been different
but when it's good, it's good and he's
good
so he touched me

ok!
i let him touch me
only i didn't see it coming,
then it was too late to realize and now
he's touching me

my instinct is to run
but
he touched me and now i can't let go
he touched my heart and now i can't let
go, but don't tell him, i don't want him
to know

a good man

i had a good man

one that cradled my soul
at night i counted his warm kisses as i
put out that unwanted light

in the morning i woke to the glow of his
eyes and all day sat between the
solitude of his thighs

a good man

when he wasn't running around with
some chicks or when his boys and them
don't got his head flipped

a good man

when his shit is tight or when he ain't
accusing me of some shit he thinks i did
because he wasn't around on some
random night

his love sold my soul with all its secrets
waiting to reveal its self and unfold
it touched me on the inside multiplied
by ten!
made me sing again
it sliced leaving pain that only he
dressed and hid

a good man

when he wasn't fucking some whore in my bed
when he ain't filling lies up in my head
or hooking up with my friend
or forgetting that we have a beginning and want to talk about how we could end

he was a good man

and i showed him that i could be just as good as him
and i fucked his friend

when it's time

if he could move me with his tongue
speaking words of wisdom
when he'd shimmer, I'd shine
there's no waste of time
rhythmic bodies intertwine
my lips dipped in wine

his words fondle me as our thighs create parallel
lines
where his becomes mine,
where i scream out
for penetration but its not the time

cat and mouse at play
cookies and cream
strawberries and milk
our bodies move like black soft silk
moist mouths ride down
hard hips rise up,
it's the sweetest juice to fill up your cup

in
out
down
up
sweet... he moves
sweet soft touches as he moves
teasing stroking my cat
keeping me at bay
his lips feel

touch and caress me
his words fondle me
as our thighs create parallel lines
where his becomes mine
where i beg for penetration but it's not the time

he carries me away
unwrapping me like a chocolate kiss
licking before he eats
dividing me like a cream filled cookie
eating the cream first
playing with me then dipping me
in his tall glass of milk
penetration!

wake up
by ralph ingrassia jr

flags red and blue
symbolizing the organization
of a crew
kids of all ages not knowing
what they do
to them this is life, to them
this is right
no responsible parents to
keep them focused
only the streets that leave
them broken

        their words become a graveyard
    full of everlasting funerals, everyday's hard

                days become shorter,
                 nights become colder
                  the day they joined
         was the day they sold their soul
                       over
        no goals, no achievements,
               no one to push,
                   have faith,
               or believe in them
    criminal mindset takes place,
shunning any reflection
that will reveal their true face
robbery outbreaks
              because oh!
              the shortage of food
              and water,
              killings of sons and
              daughters
              is this what life has to offer?
              we are imprisoned

58

imbedded in sin and corruption
drugs money and gun busting
no more tubman's, douglass's, or
mr king's

    black people wake up the alarm will ring!

talking in his sleep

i felt his lips move
i heard his mind
it laughed
as sleep woke him in the night
as life dawned on him
as truth represented him
as i sat and listened

there he took my words
kidnapped my dreams
and gave it all back in the form of a puzzle
i heard him cry
as he killed we
and called out for someone other than me

when morning came, truth left him
and lies returned to comfort him
i understood
i held him in my arms
caressed him with my inner thigh
i gave him a warm dark place to lay down his lies

i could feel it in his hands
taste it on his tongue
and smell it on his lips
it grew stronger and stronger inside of me
it was the vague sent of infidelity

but i didn't hold my voice and cried out with joy as he placed his lies deeper inside

life became new
the skies that were grey where now blue, and time that was lost came back not a moment too soon to save me

maybe i could have controlled it but it was my heart and it was he who stole it
so when it was all said and the lies were done

so were we

the b49 after love

un-confident i stand wet
from the rain splashing on
my forehead
alone in a mist of rubbish
un-confident, i take four
steps towards my destination

eyes blazing
eyes stirring within, heat
burning holes through me
from inside,
somewhere from inside
inside i loudly scream
stop!!

left unheard
unsound
unmoved
unconfident

un-confident i stand afraid to
sit
i alone stand afraid to sit
i alone stand in a sea of
bodies
brushing against me as they
pass
hustling to rest

i anticipate
wait for my arrival

"flatbush"
the driver bellows
below the steps from the
open door there i stand
un-confident

i've been your means

here i am it's me
sitting where i always sit
here where i always am
you probably don't even see me, but
that's all right
it really doesn't matter at this point
yet i can't help but wonder is it
because it's me?

i know i am not what you wanted
but i have always been just what you
need, haven't i?
i am that cold glass of wine sliding
down your throat
that long awaited herb

or even
a casual smoke
i have been that stiff drink
jack dan
jim bean
haven't i been your every means?

i can take you a way make you forget
today there is no hurt when you're
inside of me
why don't you take a sip, it's me

here i am it's me
sitting where i always sit
here where i always am
you probably don't even see me, but
that's all right
if you don't want to take a sip
i'll be here when you slip

when i felt love

i look to the sun
darkness still finds me
retro aspects of life confine me
the drudgery of fact and fiction
orange colored leaves
tall weeping trees
mountains that call
birds full of song
doe eyes wondering in the dark
wilderness at bay asking me to
please stay

still i look to the sun and
darkness finds me
a breath small and moist
one touch wraps my body
delicately fondling my soul
he moves to enter
"shhhh"
i'm told
and i look to the sun
it still finds me

just an obscurity, what can he be?
like a gentle breeze he passes through me
a touch i have long forgotten
he summons me
although he may not know
yet i only wonder if i should stay
or go

he runs through my veins,
maybe too free
vigorously
like God blowing the leaves
from a tree
and i feel him
my torso on air shivering in fear

He mutters words that ring
bitter sweet in my mind
but still he is kind
and i accept as if he could ever
be mine
and darkness finds me

to only hear his voice makes my
world still
and his smile
is a void that has been filled
but his touch!
makes all the passion in me run
wild

he climbed inside me
a sweet melody plays
i play
but i am not free
i feel the torment of love as it
blows, the earth moves
and i could see life as it grows

i moved
the night i fell in love

the sound of goodbye:
never chosen

he said that he had something to say
but he wanted to do it in that maxwell
sumthing, sumthing sweet kind of way

and well what could i say
he carried flowers in the right hand
sweet on his lips
and lust in the left while he undressed me
and rubbed my hips

yeah my baby had something he had to say

with his tongue he licked me from my lips
to my lower hips
with his hands, he studied my body
 like it was God's master plan
and all i kept thinking is "dear Lord this is
my man"

he tasted every inch of me
and he told me to cum
but he wasn't done
so he held me down on the bed and told me
"don't run"
his body moved into me,
his legs wrapped around me
and his hands held me close

the tears rolled down his eyes
and he got a quick shiver in his thighs
but i know the sound of goodbye
always special,
but never the special one
always the best
but just not the best one
passionate and sexy
but never enough
great woman,
but only for a fuck

never really noticed
or not noticed at all
never loved for long
even when i've given my all
always left broken with hurt unspoken

never giving in to never being chosen

www.ingramcontent.com/pod-product-compliance
Lightning Source LLC
LaVergne TN
LVHW091318080426
835510LV00007B/545